W9-AAX-305

Free Verse Editions

Edited by Jon Thompson

13 ways of happily

books 1 & 2

Emily Carr

Parlor Press
Anderson, South Carolina
www.parlorpress.com

**Vincennes University
Shake Learning Resources Center
Vincennes, In 47591-9986**

812.6
C 311+
2011

Parlor Press LLC, Anderson, South Carolina

© 2011 by Parlor Press
All rights reserved.
Printed in the United States of America
S A N: 2 5 4 - 8 8 7 9

Library of Congress Cataloging-in-Publication Data

Carr, Emily, 1978-
  13 ways of happily : books 1-2 / Emily Carr.
      p. cm. -- (Free verse editions)
   ISBN 978-1-60235-202-5 (pbk. : alk. paper) -- ISBN 978-1-
60235-203-2 (adobe ebook)
   I. Title. II. Title: Thirteen ways of happily. III. Series.

PS3603.A77265A616 2011
811'.6--dc22

                                        2010054542

Cover design by David Blakesley.
Cover image: "Happiness" by Emily Carr. Oil on paper. Image
U990.17.1-2 courtesy of University of Victoria Art Collections.

Printed on acid-free paper.

Parlor Press, LLC is an independent publisher of scholarly
and trade titles in print and multimedia formats. This book is
available in paper, cloth and Adobe eBook formats from Parlor
Press on the World Wide Web at http://www.parlorpress.com or
through online and brick-and-mortar bookstores. For submission
information or to find out about Parlor Press publications, write
to Parlor Press, 3015 Brackenberry Drive, Anderson, South
Carolina, 29621, or e-mail editor@parlorpress.com.

contents

For B.C.

There is no story in which you
are not the background.

13 ways of happily

book 1: the journal of elastic perception.

Getting married is like that.
Getting married is not like that.

—Marie Ponsot "The Border"

draft 1, eye, white & spring.

1

the young housewife forging myth in the kitchen—like all
the old hopes, the beginning can only be called by what it is not

2

something *panting*—truly—in this ecstatic
anarchic release into the commonplace: the very thing (as foetus) &
   object

of enjoyment (amore propre) disoriented in the whitehot air

3

            —yes everyday falling while gravity
throws apples from the trees—

4

in which version did we—
a woman   (double you'd
        a child   (so microscopically correct
                a man   (practices yes, no—
share that single cell?

5

      in the leaf & bud & how the blue
swings swagger from cowboy
          hats sparrows make happy dustbaths—

6

try to be patient. high above the old white

         pinwheels in
the dilated gaze of sublet
           the sparrow's eye, leafless—
       with bewildered adjacency

7

as it falls: unchristened unclarified every
hour accidental a child & a chicken play tag in flight from the
everchanging it—.

8

—decaying now in finemilk
                       foam of sea the dream traces
a hand-picked wingbone unfading wax flowers

9

                                     it's from this wound you first emerged
oblivious in excess fish in the air begging for sea soul in the gap
between

10

yes there is no one
to tell you for years you will fall, in
                   a gradual reenactment—.

11

listen. like wings sprouting in the mind the bonepile grows

12

                   but these are very real, very precise
butterflies all-mond brown & a-mind white an ecstasy of
crystalline palimpsest wobbling across wheatfields swayed—like
skyscrapers or trees

13

from time to time do we all
go through this dissolve root to leaf
of now intimate at last, on the tremolo
near wingtip

after J. Retallack

draft 2, & you know this is your fate to waver.

1

                on a rainspun afternoon when bombs
        fall a continent away the season

flimmers like a watery jewel on the dream's
            cobweb & the sparrow of what you are wakes, this
        slaphappy derelict—

2

in the empty ballfield the rockies' chalk
               outline dissolves choked with chickweed
       & wildradish the fatslush rain is trying to explain—.

3

forget about venetian blinds, slip
through that window: spilling like thick blonde milk a solo
                                        joy note

4

crumpled spandex sun carmurder
                        noise dioxidedrunk magnolia & soon too

sparrow chorus

5

        Christ whatever this strange hopeful fever:
in the mountains violets have broken
      the rocks inaccurate grasses keep a feckless guard—

6

  self conscious with beauty & food, a sobbing frog leapt from
that generous pond

7

       in dazzling subdivisions where no
tree grows a she in loslung pants & spaghetti
strap zigzag catwalks utterly lost
          in the morning hope of meat

8

(you do not
know which to prefer: the shadows of
lifesized fiberglass cows or the child with a
plush octopus, barking

9

aimless wasteful & drunk the sun is lunatic logic but lovely yes like
lemonjuice

10

but world is one short,
& you in your generous
bed are the last astonishing
mammal in whirligig slomotion from the dream

you are coming back through—

11

wheeling out of your ordinary
thighs through curtains & cloud yeast

the fine young season flails screes skirls
a mirage of buoyant polyglot—.

12

       nearby by accident, green mountains melt
like jello in slo liberation the world turns on its stem

13

        (you too are wavering you are careless
volunteering your seed—

after J. Kyger

draft 3, the flower of having passed through paradise in a dream.

1

something
[dueling in
a drop of
water
below a layer
of scum]
reaches us
from the
deepest
realities:
the marine
world…

2

take out your pen./   begin./
                        with the terrible gaze of songbirds
two elderly drunks stare at the girl

in the pepsi ad wasps fly noiseless through chandeliers
the arc admits its powerlessness,
                                              /& God.

3

today, as yesterday, a stallion rolls in a pasture
of blue ether & we are his/tory's human hands

4

... each moment of grief & surprise overwhelmed by an immense
swarm of invisible—

5

phyto
plankton
in a raindrop
echo &
expire swim
ming in sky

6

sparrows
gossip an
angel
irridiates
from a
lobster
coloured
curb
saying
America begins
here   p.s.
so lonely
blooming

7

       in spring riots of sparrow the child
boobytraps a bulldozer taffeta cannas/   toss fistfuls of
   rain on beautiful grasses, where they are broken

8

exuberant, wet a newspaper lifts
     its broken wing shadows drip from treeflesh
mitochondria evaporate, shredding sun

9

space voyages report nothing. nothing, nothing—

10

soaring
over a
neon
water
fall a tin &
broken
blemish
on the
sky's
backwash
the end a
billboard
proclaims
of the
rainbow

11

… the dandelion bites
its tongue on the
green hardness grow
ing inside against
the hum of luminous
doves you strain forward,
hoping…

12

brilliant, scalped dreaming the hero's sleep—a god who made, it
said, the world

13

              which way would you have come this
way, delirious & shredded sailing sideways through the
greenly ravished vowels

after F. Ponge

book 2, an alphabet of gluing from misshapen wings.

The curious, sings.

—*Erin Moure*

draft 4, the long fall to dirt heaven.

1

the colonel of a paradisetree whips in
wind like a train

over violets, waving to whatever
down there he thinks is a god

2

in the heaven of June, a naked angel scratches
a mosquito bite checks her

watch at wits end the limp guilloutined gladioli are
radiant & lonely singing in disbelief—

3

the sun is molten lookingglass masquerading in the foil of
every kind of tree

4

you are of three minds: like elegant grasshoppers
          tearing each other to pieces in the unleavened
    dandelions dreaming
                    of someone not born
               yet someone who will change
               your life—

5

in marvelous bones of bermudagrass & whiteclover, where

a blue bullet decomposes our
        god the father on a rainbow gallops horseless

6

the skypelt makes its last great sentence

          cosmos buds throw a
          pantomime of pink over the
          tiny graves
      the rain opens in his tracks

7

        ants carry bread in their mouths across
the immense & fertile grasses. the light is gorgeous & they are
so quick—

8

think now of all the splendor of the ethereal: angels &
cricketfrogs
                        making beautiful clatter, children
bright as pickup sticks
                                    in their wet clothes
screaming through dead constellations

9

someone has invented happily
solemnly hunting or flapping like busy flamingos
in the flatlands of beauty

10

god's a contraction in the plot, like salt
grains drying on the neck's edge of sea—

11

                  on stained glass sheep accumulate
in a few cramped words vineyards
vanish into lime

the garden takes residence in three veiled women addicted
to prayer

12

so that we may pretend what is ephemeral is permanent—
           the child's orbit collapses.
christ's exhaustion glisters among enormous applauding
roses...

13

when the breath of the living shaves the season's bloodred
comb the sun is strapped to witness…

after M. Ruefle

draft 5, half a wishbone expressing with broken breast the truth.

1

bouncing whitely off metal & chrome the child scrambles
through hope's detritus a beautiful geometry of adverb &
bone

2

        already you hear what the blood is saying
to the heart: neither ape nor angel

3

across stationwagons & training
wheels the mute skeletons of wooden pirates
plastic fish deboned deep

fried chickens a chanel billboard is softclicking—

4

                              (with her gluedon
                oncorhynchus scales silt eyes & ears & larger-
          than-life the mermaid interlaces ambition &
          ephemeral—.

5

           in its spilled blaze indignant &
      singular, a rainbow flails with its peculiar
      vibrato pi unfurls…

6

quaking almond children demand large hamburgers, their
shadows go on pulling one thing toward/   another

7

it is the 4th of July. you are smoking silvathins
      heat paddles across the brown drink in a happy
           glass. already you wanted to leave.
already you are letting go…

8

you see how
easy it is…
the lonely
hero
flings
herself to
watery
delirium
bobs out
broken up
& up, this
ruptured
insane
voluptuous
ness—

9

       overspilling the water's charred silk: woosey sun,
white nunca, red meat, this bright hydrogen as/if
                                 flimmering

10

       like calculus never arriving at any
promised heaven gravity erases the seams

11

             the pool goes on, islands of chryselephantine
sky —this is happening it has in fact/   (without you
           —everything does—

12

from which singing must come:
love is blank, broken, a sail at the end of the world…

13

(a glossalia of sloppy blonde your ruined hope flowers

after R. Johnson

draft 6, dandelion to the instant.

1

we come into the world & there it is
    makeshift, first/person time & wish enmeshed a severed
        hand absorbing the (fruit) trees

2

       words curve backwards like bluelight filtering through
a keyhole… or like a shoal of junebugs serrating

inverted worlds of hotviolet & rippling enamelgreen

3

                    among great sopping fists & slanty wobbling
            wings of tree, noon is atoms
                                    alive, joyous & improbable

4

next to diet dinners & silverqueen a butchered calf sings—.

5

the murdered world infuses everything. the murdered world is
here now.

           (the only question is what,
      before the god became a god who, it said,
      called—

6

                              wet &
                    senselessly beautiful.—
                    treebone palimpsests
                    the concrete.—
                    trashblown. but the
                    sky is triumphant,
                    pinwheeling.—

7

                    o louvre of the world, inhabited once
          by apes, snowy egrets disintegrating, a sundrunk bulldozer,
          gods rippling in the hotcoloured air…

8

the minnow—exhausted, singing on the surface of its human
—surrenders

9

turned inside out beyond their own nerves, your bones are
hollering...

10

       this *is* tomorrow.
            scissors & silverware, a camouflage
            pencil.

the fruit trees & fragments are politely unraveled but no meal
has been prepared

11

       ——

         your family eats quickly from trays
     silent insane insects shred venetian

     the child bruises, & steps out of the
     room
       ——

         forever undressing & undreaming,
     sometimes walking in that crowd you become
     it…

12

treemind pushes out of window frame like a flame,
the storm clouds are speeding, extravagant, unnecessary…

(missing a hand & one part of a wing

13

which one are you/   & who would know—.

after J. Williams

acknowledgments

Earlier versions of some of these poems were published in *CV2, Margie*, and *Free Verse*, & as part of my doctoral dissertation, *to loot to hew & Eden*.

Many thanks to the Canadians & ex-patriot Americans who shepherded me through the writing of these poems: Tom Wayman, Erin Wunker, Mike Roberson, Kirsten Pullen, Susan Bennett, Robert Majzels, Daphne Marlatt, & Sina Queyras. And to my lovely parents who let me drop out of medical school to be a poet: thank you.

about the author

Emily Carr's first book, *directions for flying* (Furniture Press), was the winner of the 2009 Furniture Press Poetry Prize. Her chapbook, *the story will fix you it is there outside your &*, was published in Toadlily Press's 2009 Quartet Series. In 2010, Emily was a Poetry Fellow at the Vermont Studio Center & Writer in Residence at the Jack Kerouac House. You can read her work in recent issues of *Prairie Schooner, The Spoon River Poetry Review, Hayden's Ferry Review, The Journal, Bombay Gin, Margie, Interim, Caketrain, Phoebe, Fourteen Hills, The Capilano Review, So To Speak, dusie,* and *Versal.*

Photograph of Emily Carr by Brad Carr. Used by permission.

Free Verse Editions

Edited by Jon Thompson

CPSIA information can be obtained at www.ICGtesting.com
Printed in the USA
BVOW011838250911

272034BV00002B/59/P